HARMONY
❋ ❋ ❋
the Honey Bee

Joel & Pippa Pixley

Published by the Co-operative College 2014

www.co-op.ac.uk

Holyoake House, Hanover Street, Manchester M60 0AS

ISBN: 978-0-85195-336-6

Written and illustrated by Joel & Pippa Pixley

Printed by RAPSpiderweb

In the heart of the hive, all hustle and bustle,

Harmony the honey bee had tidied her room —

all by herself!

In the hive there were always **lots** of jobs to be done. Harmony wanted to help feed her baby brothers and sisters.

She went to the storeroom and picked up

some bee bread . . .

and carried it
towards the nursery . . .

. . . but there were **hundreds** of hungry babies waiting for their breakfast!

Harmony the honey bee was only very little.

She thought the job was a bit too BIG!

A funny bee called Hatty saw that
Harmony needed help.

The two bees
had a great time
throwing and catching.

~~ ✻✻✻ ~~

This job may be big,
but we can get it done,
If we work together,
we can even make it fun!

~~ ✻✻✻ ~~

Harmony felt so pleased that all the babies were fed,
but in the hive there were always **lots** of jobs to be done . . .

Harmony and Hatty wanted to help build a new honeycomb to store their favourite food.

Hatty tried one way. . .

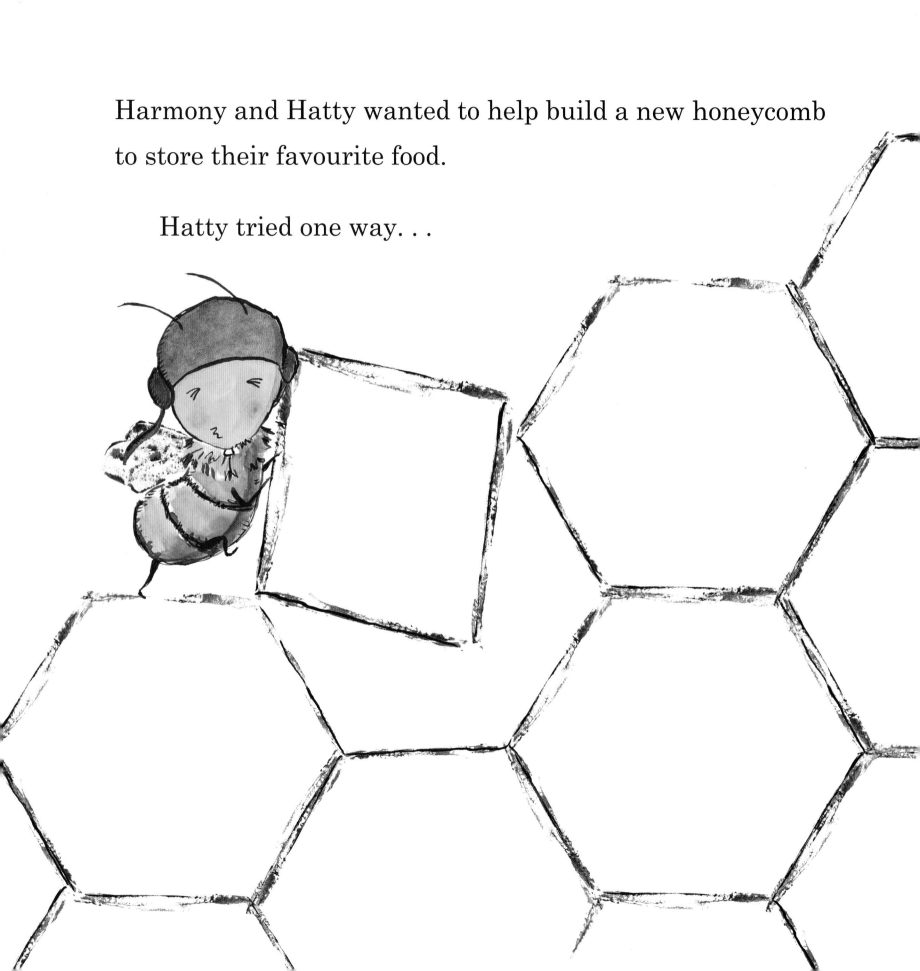

and Harmony tried
another way. . .

. . . but it **just**
wasn't working!

Harmony the honey bee was only very little.
She thought the job was a bit too *Tricky!*

A busy bee called Hazel saw that they needed help.

They all had a great time as they stuck the pieces together with lots of gloopy glue.

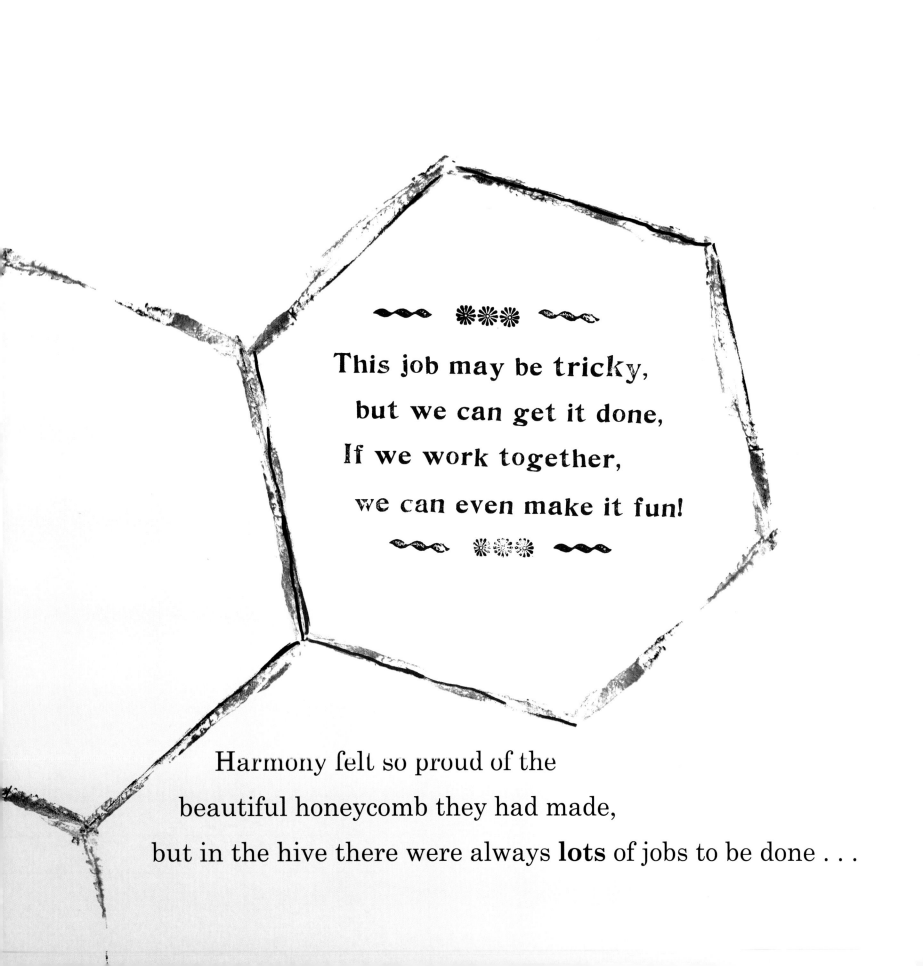

This job may be tricky,
but we can get it done,
If we work together,
we can even make it fun!

Harmony felt so proud of the
beautiful honeycomb they had made,
but in the hive there were always **lots** of jobs to be done . . .

Harmony, Hatty and Hazel
carefully crept to the door of the hive.
It was their turn to guard the honey stores.

They had never seen the bright world outside before.

It looked so **dazzling** and **dangerous!**

Harmony the honey bee was only very little.

She thought the job was a bit too **scary!**

An old bee called Tatty saw that they needed help.

She showed them how to flap their wings so fast that they made an exciting noise . . .

buzZZ!

This job may be scary,
but we can get it done,
If we work together,
we can even make it fun!

Harmony, Hatty and Hazel felt amazing . . .

... as they buzzed into the sunshine.

They were so busy circling and swooping and laughing . . .

. . . that they hadn't noticed the **hungry weasel**
slinking sneakily towards
the hive!

Harmony the honey bee was only very little,
but she remembered how her friends had helped her
with the **big** job of feeding all the babies . . .

and with the **tricky**
job of building the
new honeycomb . . .

and with the
scary job of
learning to fly!

This job may be big,
   but we can get it done,
It's tricky and it's scary,
   but we don't have to run!

If we work together,
   we can even make it fun!
Buzz, buzz, buzZZZ
Come on everyone!

The bees buzzed so **loudly** . . .

buzZZ

. . . that the weasel was scared away by the **big** noise!

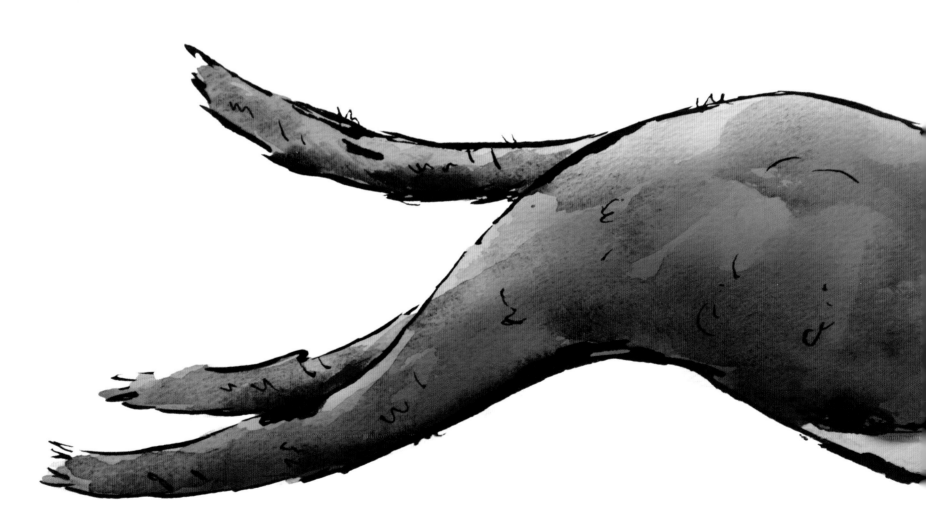

In the heart of the hive, all hustle and bustle,

Harmony enjoyed a honey supper . . .

. . . **together with all her friends!**

Bees are not the only creatures who know how to work together. People are really good at working together, too. When they help each other they can do amazing things!

A long time ago, in the year 1844, a group of people in a town called Rochdale had some very big problems. They didn't have much money and the shopkeepers sold them dirty food which made their children poorly. By working together they set up their own shop where people in the town could buy really good food. It was called a Co-operative Society.

Since then lots of other people have co-operated to start shops, factories, schools, farms, and to build houses to make their lives better.

You can still visit the Rochdale Pioneers' first shop which is now a museum.

Throughout history many co-operatives have used the beehive as a symbol because these tiny insects have so much to teach us about the benefits of working together. Bee images can be found on co-operative buildings, banners, and in books and adverts.

Bees make "bread" from different flavours and colours of pollen!
✳✳✳

All the worker bees in the hive are female!
〰 ✳✳✳ 〰

They work together to build honeycomb using wax that comes from glands on their bodies!

The Co-operative Heritage Trust is a registered charity *(charity number 1121610)* founded in 2007 by the Co-operative Group, Co-operatives UK and the Co-operative College to safeguard the movement's unique and irreplaceable heritage. The Trust's mission is:

"To inspire people within and beyond the co-operative movement about the origins, development and contemporary relevance of co-operation by collecting, safeguarding and making accessible artefacts and documentation through lifelong learning and research."

The Co-operative Heritage Trust is custodian of the Rochdale Pioneers Museum (the building where the Pioneers commenced trading on 21 December 1844) and also of the National Co-operative Archive, which holds 200 years of co-operative records. The Co-operative College manages the Museum and Archive on behalf of the Trust.

To find out more about the Rochdale Pioneers go to **www.rochdalepioneersmuseum.coop/**
and visit the Co-operative Heritage Trust's website **www.co-operativeheritage.coop/**

The story of Harmony the Honey Bee has been generously supported by:

Heritage Lottery Fund, Esmée Fairbairn Foundation, John Paul Getty Junior Foundation